SIGNSPOTTING III

LOST AND LOSTER IN TRANSLATION

Compiled by Doug Lansky

A PERIGEE BOOK

A PERIGEE BOOK
Published by the Penguin Group
Penguin Group (USA) Inc.

375 Hudson Street, New York, New York 10014, USA
Penguin Group (Canada), 90 Eglinton Avenue East, Suite 700, Toronto,
Ontario M4P 2Y3, Canada (a division of Pearson Penguin Canada Inc.)
Penguin Books Ltd., 80 Strand, London WC2R 0RL, England
Penguin Group Ireland, 25 St. Stephen's Green, Dublin 2, Ireland
(a division of Penguin Books Ltd.)
Penguin Group (Australia), 250 Camberwell Road, Camberwell,
Victoria 3124, Australia (a division of Pearson Australia Group Pty. Ltd.)
Penguin Books India Pvt. Ltd., 11 Community Centre, Panchsheel Park,
New Delhi—110 017, India
Penguin Group (NZ), 67 Apollo Drive, Rosedale, North Shore 0632,
New Zealand (a division of Pearson New Zealand Ltd.)
Penguin Books (South Africa) (Pty.) Ltd., 24 Sturdee Avenue, Rosebank,
Johannesburg 2196, South Africa

Penguin Books Ltd., Registered Offices: 80 Strand, London WC2R 0RL,
England

While the author has made every effort to provide accurate telephone
numbers and Internet addresses at the time of publication, neither
the publisher nor the author assumes any responsibility for errors, or
for changes that occur after publication. Further, the publisher does
not have any control over and does not assume any responsibility for
author or third-party websites or their content.

First edition: September 2009

Library of Congress Cataloging-in-Publication Data

Signspotting III : lost and loster in translation / compiled by Doug
Lansky.
    p.   cm.
"A Perigee book."
ISBN 978-0-399-53522-2
1. Signs and signboards—Pictorial works. 2. Billboards—Pictorial
works. 3. Travel—Humor. 4. Photography, Humorous. I. Lansky,
Doug. II. Title: Signspotting 3. III. Title: Sign spotting three.
    GT3910.S54   2008
    659.13'42—dc22   2009008700

PRINTED IN MEXICO

10 9 8 7 6 5 4 3 2 1

Most Perigee books are available at special quantity discounts for
bulk purchases for sales promotions, premiums, fund-raising, or
educational use. Special books, or book excerpts, can also be created
to fit specific needs. For details, write: Special Markets, Penguin Group
(USA) Inc., 375 Hudson Street, New York, New York 10014.

INTRODUCTION

It's hard to imagine a world without signs. No stop signs, no arrows, no speed limits, no warnings. No bright colors screaming for your attention. Take a good look next time you step outside—signs are virtually everywhere. In the county of Kent, England, alone (presumably the only county that bothered to count), they discovered they had 140,000 signs.

But do we really need them—any of them? In 2007, the west German town of Bohmte (pop. 13,000) decided to remove all of their signs and street markings. They even took away the curbs, sidewalks, and traffic lights. And they're paying more than 2.3 million euros to do it. Why? Because—this is true—they wanted to make their roads safer. They had tried speed traps and crosswalks—the usual fixes—but those didn't seem to keep the cars and trucks from racing through their main street, treating pedestrians and cyclists like expendable supporting characters in a video game.

Taking a page out of the reverse psychology handbook, Bohmte decided drivers were too comfortable with signs—to the point that they ignored them. By removing them, they believed drivers would get nervous and hit the brakes. The roads were remade with a burnt sienna brick to give a subtle indication that drivers were entering a special zone. "Generally speaking, what we want is for people to be confused. When they're confused, they'll be more alert and drive more carefully," Bohmte's deputy mayor Willi Ladner told the *Washington Post* just as the new system opened.

Naturally, without marked spaces, people can park as they please as long as—here comes unwritten rule number one—they don't leave them in the middle of the road. The other unwritten rules are yielding to anything coming from the right (car, bus, bike, or pedestrian) and sticking to the nationwide 30-kilometers-per-hour limit for city driving.

What happened? One eyewitness, Tony Paterson, a newspaper reporter from London's *Independent*, noted that vehicles that "pass along this stretch of sign-free road seem to be driven by swivel-headed paranoiacs with rubber vertebrae. They crawl along at little more than 15 miles per hour, their occupants constantly craning their necks to make doubly sure that they are not going to hit anything, be it a pedestrian, cyclist, or even another car."

This "shared space" concept is the work of legendary Dutch traffic engineer Hans Monderman, who wants road users to negotiate with hand signals and eye contact instead of traffic signs. ("If you treat people like idiots, they'll act like idiots," he likes to say.) In the Dutch town of Drachten, removing the signs not only reduced accidents but kept traffic more fluid and reduced fuel consumption. In Haren, another recently signless Dutch town, the number of accidents at one intersection dropped by 95 percent.

Now the European Union is subsidizing this shared-space program across the Continent. And interest is spreading worldwide.

Where does this leave signspotters? Not to despair . . . experts believe that the shared-space program works best in smaller towns (with intersections hosting less than 15,000 vehicles a day) and just for short sections of road. More than that and drivers lose patience with the concept. Besides, after paying to take away the signs, Bohmte decided to explain this new sign-free policy by—you'll never guess—putting up a sign.

LOCATION: TIRANA, ALBANIA   CREDIT: JAMES WILSON

Take Crop Patterns 101, study advanced spacecraft sightings, and take field trips to Area 51.

LOCATION: POINT REYES NATIONAL SEASHORE, CALIFORNIA, USA   CREDIT: ERIS WEAVER

Seems like the lifesaving aspect needs a bit of work.

LOCATION: NEW DELHI, INDIA   CREDIT: SANDRA KELL

Welcome to Paradise Interiors. Where we bring your decorating dreams to life.

By the Numbers
About 1 billion: Total English speakers (first, second, or third language)
882,000,000: Native Mandarin speakers
24,000–30,000: Vocabulary words of an educated native English speaker
3,000: Words used in a "working vocabulary"
300,000: English headwords in the *Oxford English Dictionary*, not including 615,000 variations of these words
225,000: Spanish words in contemporary use
100,000: French words in contemporary use
25,525: Words recognized by the lingual governing body Academié Française
89: Percent of European Union schoolchildren who study English as a foreign language
32: Percent of European Union schoolchildren who study French as a foreign language
8: Percent of European Union schoolchildren who study Spanish as a foreign language
87: Percent of Dutch who speak English
51: Percent of Germans who speak English
60: Percent of Finns who speak English

Just to be safe, you probably don't want to order a Slush Puppie here.

LOCATION: JOSHUA TREE NATIONAL PARK, CALIFORNIA, USA   CREDIT: BOB ECKER

Get that "fried liver" freshness you've been missing.

Hey, thanks for the warning!

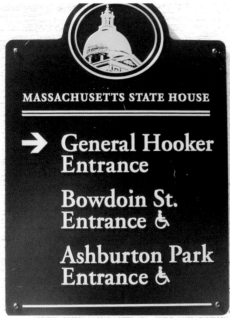

Apparently, the specialist hookers have their own entrance.

C'mon, jump in! It's not like there are giant spikes in the water specially placed to spear you in the nether regions.

Sales have been flat lately.

LOCATION: SHIMLA, INDIA   CREDIT: ERIKA ROGERS

Nice to see people taking a stand against racism—and eating outside.

Don't even think
about entering.

Welcome to the
Insane Lane.

When a pornographer takes
a day job making signs.

At least they're up-front about where the food will end up.

**СПАСАТЕЛЬНЫЙ ЖИЛЕТ
ПОД ВАШИМ КРЕСЛОМ
LIVE VEST UNDER YOUR SEAT**

سترة النجاة تحت مقعدك

In the event of an emergency, please beat your live vest to death, then put it on.

LOCATION: GLEN PARK AREA, SAN FRANCISCO, CALIFORNIA, USA   CREDIT: INGE WEIDMANN

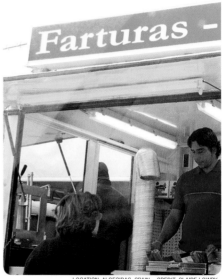

LOCATION: ALGECIRAS, SPAIN   CREDIT: CLAIRE LOWRY

Well, the ride was good while it lasted.

Nothing like the smell of fresh Farturas first thing in the morning.

The breakfast of champions.

Nothing quite says welcome like the promise of sandy balls.

LOCATION: KEMMERER, WYOMING, USA   CREDIT: CHAN WELLER

LOCATION: PORT ALBERNI, BRITISH COLUMBIA, CANADA   CREDIT: STORM CUNNINGHAM

Welcome, All Indecisive Convention Members!

If you're looking for Somass, you might try Vancouver Island.

参拝順路

USUAL ROUTE

LOCATION: NARA, JAPAN   CREDIT: SHAWN DUNNING

Two roads diverged in a wood, and I—
I took the usual route.

Is your fish getting a bit slimy? Seaweed between the scales? Extra fishy smell?
Maybe it's time to get your pet fish professionally washed.

LOCATION: GRAND RAPIDS, MICHIGAN, USA   CREDIT: MELANIE REDMAN

Ah, the perks of being the Messiah.

Presumably more profitable than the Health Valley Death Center.

LOCATION: KEY LARGO, FLORIDA, USA   CREDIT: GARY VANDEKERCKHOVE

Your leg is missing . . . SURPRISE!

Putting those welfare checks to good use.

LOCATION: BIG ISLAND, WHITEFISH LAKE, MINNESOTA, USA CREDIT: SHAINA WALKER

It's over there, on the other side of the forest.

LOCATION: GEORGIA, USA CREDIT: TOM TROCINE

You can hardly expect drivers on LSD to stick to one lane.

Suppose you should probably follow it.

LOCATION: TRANS-CANADA HIGHWAY
CREDIT: CLAIR THOMPSON

We will be checking very carefully for concealed weapons.

LOCATION: CAIRNS, AUSTRALIA
CREDIT: KRISTEN NORTON

Don't worry if you feel something slithering around your legs, trying to pull you to the bottom while swimming. Probably just an enormous octopus. Happens all the time. Enjoy the water!

LOCATION: CAPE TRIBULATION BEACH, QUEENSLAND, AUSTRALIA
CREDIT: SARAH GOOD

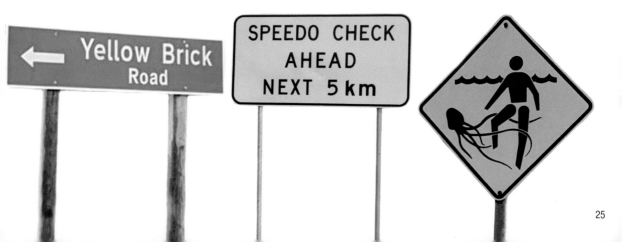

It's raining men.

**Oldies but goldies
- meals they made in Prague
100 years ago**

**Stará dobrá klasika,
aneb co se vařilo v Praze
před 100 lety**

It's not easy to cut through the famous 100-year-old top
layer of fungus on the soup, but otherwise it's not bad.

27

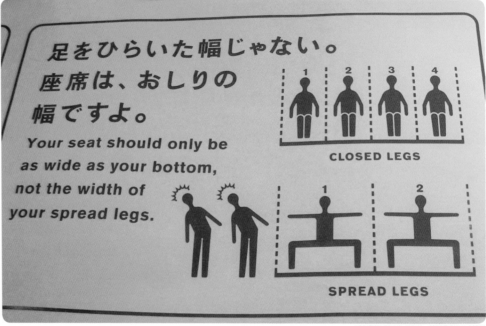

足をひらいた幅じゃない。
座席は、おしりの
幅ですよ。

**Your seat should only be
as wide as your bottom,
not the width of
your spread legs.**

CLOSED LEGS

SPREAD LEGS

Evidently, sumo warm-up exercises are also out of the question.

British Telecom has a wicked sense of humor.

LOCATION: NORFOLK, ENGLAND
CREDIT: TIM BENTINCK

LOCATION: JOHANNESBURG, SOUTH AFRICA   CREDIT: CHRISTINE AYERS

Marilyn Monroe crossing?

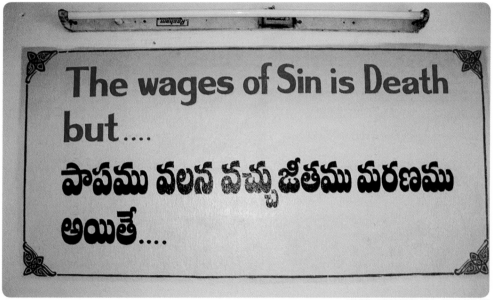

LOCATION: ANDHRA PERISH, INDIA   CREDIT: GARY COX

But what?

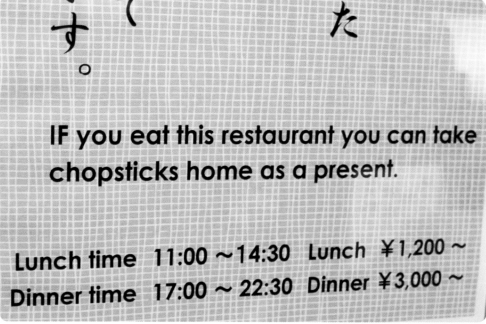

す

て

た

。

IF you eat this restaurant you can take chopsticks home as a present.

Lunch time 11:00 ~ 14:30 **Lunch** ¥1,200 ~
Dinner time 17:00 ~ 22:30 **Dinner** ¥3,000 ~

Godzilla's favorite lunch spot.

Wordspotting

English is growing. Not just the number of people who speak it, but the actual number of words. According to word analyst Paul J.J. Payack of the Global Language Monitor, there's a new word added every 98 seconds, and for the first time in history for any language, English will have passed the one million word mark by the time this book is released.

This growth is largely due to the internationalization of the language in all its variants (Chinglish, Fringlish, Snoop Dogg's "shizzle" rap language, and George W. Bush's often-quoted malapropisms such as "misunderestimate") as well as the popular spread of English itself. English as a global language may have been kick-started by the British Empire and then piggybacked a ride on the economic and cultural power of the United States, but it's now fueled and distributed largely by the Internet. As soon as new words are coined, they zip across the web with the help of sites like Urbandictionary.com. With more words and expressions that can be mangled and more English speakers to mangle them, the future of funny signs looks promising.

LOCATION: COPENHAGEN, DENMARK   CREDIT: BARBARA Z. MOSS

Sure, it's a little stuffy inside, but at least he's honest about it.

LOCATION: NATURAL BRIDGE, VIRGINIA, USA   CREDIT: RHONDA MALONEY

Coming soon! The first zoo employee born in captivity.

Possible motto: "Our customers aren't too picky."

All applicants must be at least somewhat dead.

Welcome to Community School of Excellence!!

Please repot to the Main Office

Please Repot to the Kommunity Skool of Exselence!!

LOCATION: COTTAGE GROVE, MINNESOTA, USA   CREDIT: LARRY HOLMEN

Extreme urban driving: the inverted U-turn.

Finally, a restaurant that combines the famous taste of railway
cuisine with the practicality of a stomach clinic. All for a reasonable price.

It's actually for a cooking center. Simon Cowell only vacations here.

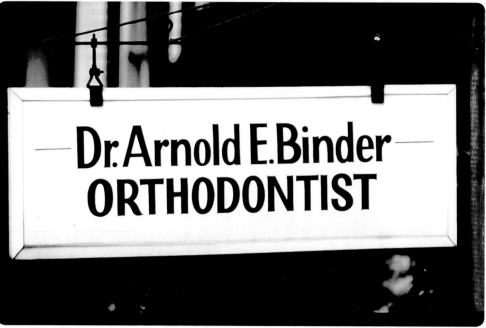

LOCATION: LITTLETON. MASSACHUSETTS. USA   CREDIT: JIM MCGRATH

Career choices were limited: It was either orthodontics, prison guard in Guantanamo, or dominatrix.

LOCATION: SOUTH ISLAND, NEW ZEALAND   CREDIT: CAROL VEESAERT

You're going the wong way.

And the Academy Award for Stick Figure in a Dramatic Pose goes to . . .

WELCOME TO
MONK CHAT
NOTE THAT: TO TALK ABOUT
- BUDDHISM
- WORLD RELIGION
- THAI CULTURE
  AND MORE

Pre-Internet chat room.

男厕所
TOILETMAN

LOCATION: BETWEEN HANGZHOU AND SHANGHAI, CHINA   CREDIT: RICHARD PATENAUDE

It's a bird. It's a plane. No, wait—it's . . .

LOCATION: GRAND CAYMAN, CAYMAN ISLANDS   CREDIT: ERICA PAGLIUCO

LOCATION: LONDON, ENGLAND   CREDIT: NICK FORESTER

For those who decide not to stop at church.

Protected by contractors.

LOCATION: NEWFOUNDLAND, CANADA   CREDIT: KATHLEEN NINNEMAN

Great moments in history: "This place
is just beautiful, and I know exactly what
I'm going to call it."

LOCATION: PALOUSE FALLS, WASHINGTON, USA   CREDIT: ANGELA D. INGALLS

There's a news flash.

Turismo

Detención para ascenso y descenso de pasajeros

Ordenanza Nº 43453

Those customs officers can get a bit frisky.

Sorry, no toilet diving.

Yes, please bring your brakeless giant truck on the highway. We'd all really appreciate that.

LOCATION: HILT, CALIFORNIA, USA
CREDIT: MARILYN HOPKINS

Welcome to bear
puppet theater!

LOCATION: MT. LEMMON, ARIZONA, USA
CREDIT: NANCY CORBETT

Finally, a country
that treats jaywalking
seriously.

LOCATION: KUWAIT CITY, KUWAIT
CREDIT: LEILA MANSOURI

Looks like it may be time
to change the town's
name.

LOCATION: ARKANSAS, USA
CREDIT: LARRY SHORTELL

تجاوز الإشارة الحمراء
يعني الموت أو السجن
Crossing the Red Signal
Leads to Death or Prison
الإدارة العامة للمرور
هندسة المرور

FIFTY SIX
POP 163

Who knew Italy had such liberal buses?

"Modern" family-planning advice.

LOCATION: NORTHAMPTON, ENGLAND
CREDIT: ADENA GOODART

LANES AVAILABLE

HoeBowl
On The Hill Lanes

SUMMER
LEAGUES
NOW
FORMING

ATM
INSIDE

Bowling for hoes.

Surround yourself with scores of retired Germans in RVs.
Enjoy our community bathrooms. We're waiting for you to visit us here in Hell.

In case of emergency

If you require assistance in evacuating your room please hang this on the outside of your door.

Forestdale Hotels

LOCATION: GLASTONBURY, ENGLAND CREDIT: PHILIP SCADDING

小心碰头
Caution: Run into It

LOCATION: DAI VILLAGE, SOUTHERN CHINA CREDIT: PEGGIE WORMINGTON

For the occupant who can get to the door and open it, but who just can't work up the energy to evacuate.

Go on, what are you waiting for?
Run into it.

Impressive . . . an entire building devoted to just one aging body part.

Apparently, one should never cut the stream of urine. At least not with giant scissors.

That whole "up" and "down" business is pretty confusing stuff.

When in use, this sign will look totally different.

LOCATION: COMMERCE CITY, COLORADO, USA   CREDIT: JOHN MCLAUGHLIN

Just don't go there.

Chinese hospitality aimed at the short-term visitor.

～　喫煙されるお客様へ　～
構内は禁煙になっております、
外の喫煙コーナーでお願いします。

Building asks a smoked visitor
in the outside smoking section
that you cannot smoke in.

LOCATION: HAKONE, JAPAN   CREDIT: FRANK MCLARNON

In short, "No Smoking."

LOCATION: SHENNONG STREAM, CHINA   CREDIT: ANDREW FOGG

In case you were thinking of . . .

この洗面台では、髪を洗ったり
洗濯等をしないで下さい。

NOTICE

No washing hair or clothes
in the toilet please.

You know us tourists, always jamming our heads
into the toilet or using the water to wash our clothes.

There's a special on half-eaten hamburgers.

LOCATION: FARMINGTON, NEW MEXICO, USA   CREDIT: CAROLYN FOX

Oddly, porn rentals are down this month.

Crossing for those with
jeans is up ahead.

LOCATION: AL UDEID, QATAR
CREDIT: RICK KUEHN

Please help us save these priceless
thousand-year-old relics and also
this cheap stainless-steel railing.

LOCATION: BEIJING, CHINA
CREDIT: PAUL BOLDING

Most of us thought this
had been banned, at least
in public.

LOCATION: ST. HELENS, MERSEYSIDE, ENGLAND
CREDIT: RAY BISHOP

保护文物
HELP PROTECT THE CULTURAL RELICS
爱护栏杆
HELP PROTECT THE RAILINGS

中国人寿 敬赠
CHINA LIFE

Gully Sucking
In
Progress

The former address of the emperor's toilet

LOCATION: IMPERIAL PALACE, CHENGDE, CHINA   CREDIT: SHARON OPPEGARD

The other crown jewels.

DO NOT

BEND, BORROW, BREAK, CUT, CLEAVE, CLIP, CRUSH,
DIVIDE, ENDANGER, HARM, MUTILATE, PARE, PINCH,
PICK, PLUCK, PULL, SEVER, SNIP, SNAP OFF, STEAL,
TAKE, TOUCH, TWIST OFF OR REMOVE

THE FLOWERS AND PLANTS

BY ORDER
RESIDENT ADMINISTRATOR

Try to find a loophole in this horticultural directive.

Bitte nicht im Stehen pinkeln ! Take a seat please !
Celui qui s'assied ne se mouille pas les pieds !

Women of the world unite!

LOCATION: OAK CREEK, WISCONSIN, USA   CREDIT: RON CLONE

Take away all the tailgate slamming and vibrators and what else is there to do?

LOCATION: CLIFFS OF MOHER, IRELAND   CREDIT: PETER HEELAN

"Hey, Mom, look how close to the edge I can get!"

74

LOCATION: ROME, OREGON, USA   CREDIT: ELLEN FINDLAY HERDEGEN

Maybe it's an ad for a nasal spray.

LOCATION: DUBLIN, IRELAND   CREDIT: LINDA E. BURG

LOCATION: PISA, ITALY (INSIDE THE LEANING TOWER OF PISA)   CREDIT: PHILIP KOOPMAN

Thank God, that bicycle was killing me.

Beware of break-dancing!

Not sure if this is a bath you'd want to take.

Finally, a transgender bathroom.

温馨提示
为避免水溅出
请您拉上浴帘

The Sweet Hint
In order not to the water splashes please pull up the bath curtain

小心地滑
Be careful! Landslide

As if one didn't already have enough to think about while doing one's business in a Chinese bathroom.

LOCATION: BATHROOM IN THE REDWALL HOTEL, BEIJING, CHINA
CREDIT: HENRIK HANSON

Signfixing

Signs may not be disappearing anytime soon, but some of the funniest ones are.

English-speaking countries are cracking down on bad signage. A new multibillion-dollar airport terminal can expect to spend more than $10 million on signage and $1.5 million in signage consulting fees. These sign consultants or "wayfinders" like David Roberts of Carter & Burgess Inc. face more issues than you might think. Aside from clearing up confusing directions to gates and luggage carousels (or lack thereof), they need to figure out whether signs should be multilingual, and if so, which language should come first. Then there are the competing interests: the airport executives want clear signage that maximizes passenger flow; the airport maintenance crew wants easy-care signs (that is, no lightbulbs or extra pieces); the airport architects want signs that don't detract from their design; the airport lawyers want signs that avoid liability; and on top of that, the wayfinders, like David Roberts, want consistency. There shouldn't be, for example, one restroom with "bathroom" on the door and another with the word "toilet." Suddenly it doesn't seem like such a cushy job.

For the signs that have been "fixed" already, this series of Signspotting books may become a historical reference. For those signs that aren't yet extinct, these books represent an endangered species list of sorts. But until every city, town, highway, shopping mall, and retail store starts employing wayfinders and setting up hotlines, it's fair to assume we can count on many more years of entertainment with new puzzling signs going up every day.

TOILET
★ LATRINE RS. 3
★ PISS RS. 2

महिला →

R LATRINE & PISS

सूचना
शौचालये भित्र कुनै पनि सामान राख्न मनाही छ!
अनावश्यक गफ गर्न यहाँ नबस्दिनुहोला।

WOMEN

Number 1 costs 2 and number 2 costs 3. Or, as it's also known, pay-per-poo premium.

British Waterways

← →

No fishing between arrows

LOCATION: CANAL IN THE UNITED KINGDOM   CREDIT: RUSSELL GREIG

Just to make things a little more difficult.

Meet the first stick figure porn star.

LOCATION: ISTANBUL, TURKEY   CREDIT: PETER WILKINS

The self-serve buffet breakfast is better known as the Ufuk Yourself.

Is it dancing they don't want, or that specific disco move where you point to the ceiling?

LOCATION: SAN FRANCISCO, CALIFORNIA, USA   CREDIT: JEANINE ALEXANDER

This would be a fun sign to have on the refrigerator.

LOCATION: SLOVENIA   CREDIT: A. DUCOMMUN

No self-pick escargot.

LOCATION: ROSEMEAD, CALIFORNIA, USA   CREDIT: HEATHER SHELTON

What are you waiting for?! C'mon in and try My Dung!

蟧蟹橫行是奇观
留待他人共养眼

Please do not catch the crabs

게가 모로 가는것은 기이하므로
타인의 관상용으로 남겨주십시오

STDs respond well to politeness.

LOCATION: SAN MATEO, CALIFORNIA, USA   CREDIT: LEO DUERR

Not a bad sign for a mechanic in Germany, but this sign is in California.

LOCATION: ELMINA, GHANA   CREDIT: EMILY OSBORNE

I'd like that "Hey, asshole!" style you had featured last week.

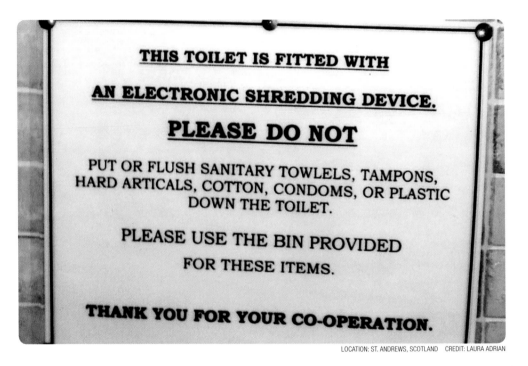

THIS TOILET IS FITTED WITH

AN ELECTRONIC SHREDDING DEVICE.

PLEASE DO NOT

PUT OR FLUSH SANITARY TOWLELS, TAMPONS, HARD ARTICALS, COTTON, CONDOMS, OR PLASTIC DOWN THE TOILET.

PLEASE USE THE BIN PROVIDED

FOR THESE ITEMS.

THANK YOU FOR YOUR CO-OPERATION.

LOCATION: ST. ANDREWS, SCOTLAND   CREDIT: LAURA ADRIAN

Introducing a toilet for thrill seekers.

LOCATION: A LIFEBOAT ON THE HOLLAND AMERICA WESTERDAM   CREDIT: ANNE OULAHAN

We thought about putting the life jackets in the rooms
or maybe in the life rafts, but there was more space in the sea.

Daily Dung—get it while it's warm!

Very Immense Person Room. Your legs must be at least ten feet long.

World food shortage inspires new themed deli.

One man's pet is another man's meal.

Even the French have a hard time swallowing this one.

LOCATION: CHINA
CREDIT: LESLEY MITCHELL

海底椰木瓜炖雪蛤膏　￥36
Braised papaya and ovary of wild frog
Айва вала кокоса seabed китайская
flowering варит затир clam снежка

98

Citizens to the right; foreign nationals and intergalactic visitors to the right.

You don't want to piss off Mom.

LOCATION: SUDBURY, MASSACHUSETTS, USA   CREDIT: JIM MCGRATH

Hey, Dad, the weirdest thing happened. I was at this
school event and my report card got burned somehow!

Dr. Latex and Dr. Coldfingers are also available.

LOCATION: EASTERN USA   CREDIT: JEFF FERENCE

Let's discuss the price outside.

Help! The keg is nearly empty!

IMATIOΘHKH

CLOA KROOM

LOCATION: ISLAND OF SANTORINI, GREECE   CREDIT: ALAN GARFIELD

Or you could hang your jacket in the cloak room.

LOCATION: LA JOLLA, CALIFORNIA, USA   CREDIT: SHANNON KELLEY

For plants trying to kick their petrochemical dependence.

LOCATION: SOMANYA, GHANA   CREDIT: PENNY PITTERSON

Sending customers "home" with love.

Potted "pot" plants or plants in a "pot"?

LOCATION: MANANG, NEPAL   CREDIT: WILLIAM BAKKER

LOCATION: BEAUNE, FRANCE   CREDIT: ANDREW LISTER

What, no yak pizza?

Finally, the moron is here.

LOCATION: TIJUANA, MEXICO CREDIT: JASON AND VALERIE PASCHEN

LOCATION: SPLIT, CROATIA CREDIT: CAITLIN THOMAS

Real-life Burning Man.

Presumably topless urination is common in this part of Croatia.

Estimado Huésped:
Colabore en mantener la playa limpia,
no tire basura.
Dear Guest:
Help us to keep clean the beach, do not
throw away the trash.

LOCATION: PUERTO SAN JOSÉ, GUATEMALA   CREDIT: KIM HANEY

Just throw it in the water.

PLEASE NOTHING IN TOILET YOU CAN'T EAT · FLUSH

LOCATION: BOAT TO GREAT BARRIER REEF, AUSTRALIA   CREDIT: JEAN SIMAT

That's setting the standards a bit high.

中国移动通信
CHINA MOBILE

可回收
RECYCLING

中国移动通信
CHINA MOBILE

不可回收
UNRECYCLING

Recycling is so 2009.

LOCATION: SLINGER, WISCONSIN, USA   CREDIT: MARINA VOBROUCEK

Even after leaving office, the former president is still contributing to greenhouse emissions.

LOCATION: STENHOUSEMUIR, CENTRAL SCOTLAND   CREDIT: STUART CRAW

One small victory: Path 1, Hiker 0.

reserved seating area
for customers with
special needs and
unaccompanied minors

LOCATION: BMI GATEWAY, HEATHROW AIRPORT, ENGLAND   CREDIT: JOHN M. SILVERBERG

Going that extra mile to pamper and tend to passengers.

Motto: "People notice when your clothes are washed by us."

Who knew you could find irony in a parking lot?

Of course, God will smite you if you try to interpret this in an impure way.

LOCATION: HO CHI MINH CITY, VIETNAM   CREDIT: MIKE BLOMGREN

How long is it?

Cannibal or pregnant lady? Either way . . .

CO SO
HUNG LONG
Chuyên GIA CÔNG CÁC LOẠI BẠC SÉC-MĂNG
BẠC MÓC CỦA HỘP SỐ VÀ PISTON CÁC LOẠI XE CƠ GIỚI
71, ĐỀ THÁM Q1
ĐT: 8372931

LOCATION: HO CHI MINH CITY, VIETNAM   CREDIT: MIKE BLOMGREN

In some countries it's okay to put up a sign about it.

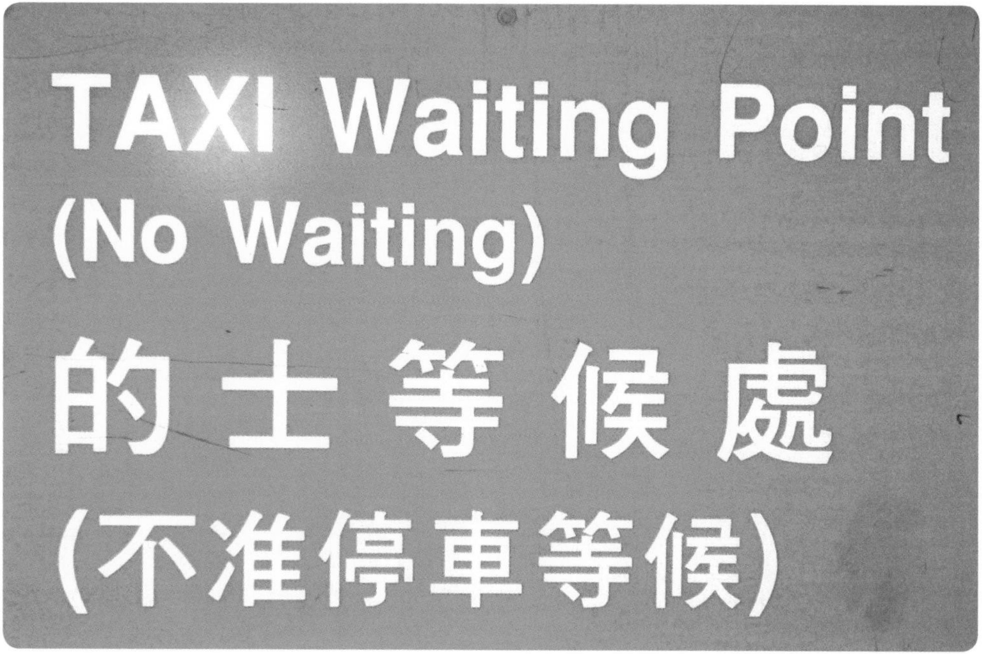

TAXI Waiting Point
(No Waiting)
的士等候處
(不准停車等候)

LOCATION: HONG KONG CREDIT: ERIK WIDMARK

You might consider the bus.

Watch out for car-eating cows.

When "Beware of Dog" doesn't provide quite enough security.

LOCATION: VIENNA, AUSTRIA   CREDIT: BARB BURCHILL

You never know when it's going to strike.

LOCATION: STAR VALLEY, ARIZONA, USA   CREDIT: SUSAN MANN

Shake those tenderloins.

Not-so-scenic overlook.

Warning: Poetic irony ahead. Very real chance you may smack your head on that "safety" and get a concussion.

LOCATION: PLITVICE JEZERA NATIONAL PARK, CROATIA   CREDIT: ANDY BALTES

No swimming allowed if you are a freakish fishman alien.

Well, obviously. You can tell by the architecture.

LOCATION: DEPARTMENT STORE IN FLORENCE, ITALY   CREDIT: KATIE ABBOTT

You never know when a body bag might come in handy.

LOCATION: HAALEM, NETHERLANDS   CREDIT: JOHN MACKESSACK

Coconuts are getting organized and they know what they want.

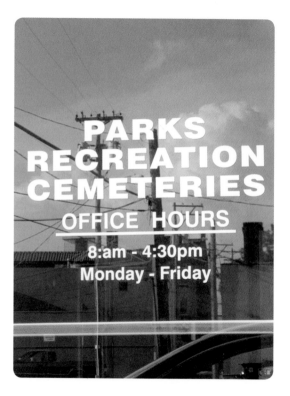

Try the new recreational cemetery: It's loads of fun. Great for the whole family.

LOCATION: RICE LAKE, WISCONSIN, USA
CREDIT: JAMES SLAUSON

Fri höjd 3,6m

LOCATION: STOCKHOLM, SWEDEN   CREDIT: DOUG LANSKY

Yep, this is the last one.

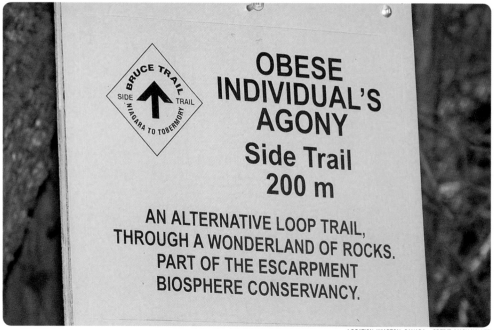

LOCATION: WIARTON, CANADA CREDIT: MARY HALLER

Bit on the heavy side? You're going to love this hike.

Nice to see feminism is finally taking hold in Mexico.

膨化食品
Crack

薯片
Chips

What legalization of drugs might look like.

主人公がポイ捨てをした。
ふるい映画だった。

The cool cowboy flicks his cigarette butt into the street. But he lives in an old movie.

HERO

VILLAIN

TOBACCO

A LONG TIME AGO

OLD MOVIE

LOCATION: TOKYO, JAPAN   CREDIT: JOHAN EKLUND

Would like to see how they diagram *The Bourne Ultimatum.*

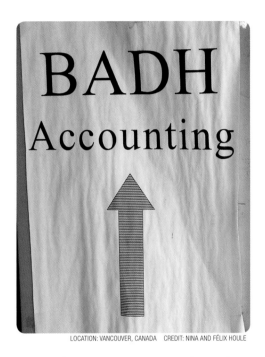

BADH
Accounting

LOCATION: VANCOUVER, CANADA   CREDIT: NINA AND FÉLIX HOULE

Royal E. Skrewd Accounting is no longer in business.

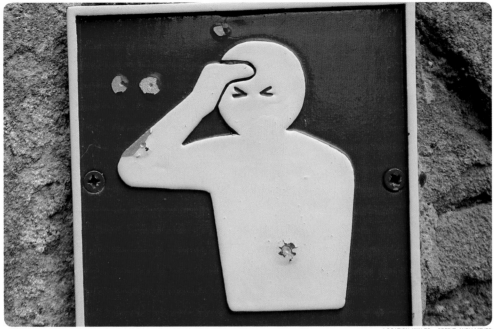

Caution: Migraine approaching.

Octopus is available at the <u>EXIT</u> of the car park

八達通付款
現可在<u>出口</u>使用

JONES LANG LASALLE.

Duh, where else would you find an octopus!

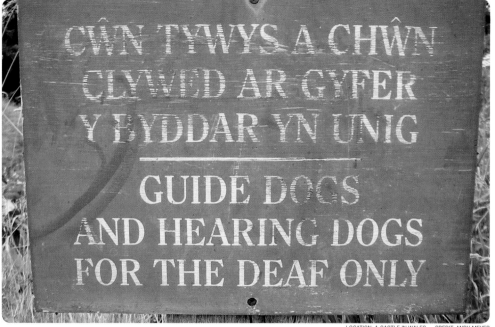

CÛN TYWYS A CHÛN
CLYWED AR GYFER
Y BYDDAR YN UNIG
_____
GUIDE DOGS
AND HEARING DOGS
FOR THE DEAF ONLY

LOCATION: A CASTLE IN WALES   CREDIT: ANDY MEYER

Blind people are screwed.

LOCATION: MEN'S RESTROOM (WHERE ELSE?) ROTORUA, NEW ZEALAND   CREDIT: BARBARA ROPER

Spit in the urinal makes it difficult to enjoy the smell and look of splattered urine.

You can eat it, kayak in it, and use it to treat inoperable cancer and stop Dutch Elm disease . . . anything!

Usually the best way to keep your shoes from getting stolen is to keep them on your feet.

LOCATION: DHARMSALA, INDIA
CREDIT: PATRICIA COLLEY

LOCATION: HONG KONG CREDIT: PAUL BOLDING

Working hard to put an end to paraphernalia once and for all.

LOCATION: HUA HIN BEACH CAFÉ, THAILAND   CREDIT: MARK PICKUP

You wouldn't want to mess up the area around a squat toilet with an unclean foot.

Electric bills getting you down? What are you waiting for?
Now's the time to switch to Porn and join millions of extremely satisfied customers.

143

If you drop that litter in the trash can, you're dead. Now slowly back away and put the garbage back on the ground where you found it. Or maybe it's the other way around. Hard to say.

LOCATION: STOCKTON, CALIFORNIA, USA   CREDIT: KAITLYN O'RINN

LOCATION: DEAD SEA, JORDAN   CREDIT: KAREN INDA

You might hurt their branches and/or feelings.

When Edvard Munch visits the Dead Sea . . .

ANOTHER LARGE ERECTION COMING SOON

www.gr...

LOCATION: JOHANNESBURG, SOUTH AFRICA   CREDIT: NELIA GUNN

Some people feel the need to announce it.

Motto: "Our name says it all."

Making Ends Meet meets its end.

LOCATION: STRATTON, ENGLAND   CREDIT: PAUL STEVENS

Er . . . yes it is.

LOCATION: ST. LUCIA CROC BREEDING CENTER, SOUTH AFRICA   CREDIT: KELLY DAIGLE

How many unattended relatives do you suppose rolled to their tragic fate before officials decided to put up this sign?

LOCATION: TRANS-CANADA HIGHWAY CREDIT: CLAIR THOMPSON

LOCATION: SANTA ROSA, CALIFORNIA, USA CREDIT: BILL LUKEROTH

Finally, a head-smashed-in buffalo jump that's handicapped accessible and has a pay phone.

To serve and protect and commit.

New spa treatment? Get papered with our new fecal face therapy.

NOTE FROM THE AUTHOR

I started photographing funny signs when, like many of you, I was caught off guard by a few signs during my travels. Now, 15 years later, I've received about 40,000 sign photos from travelers. And there are great new ones coming in every day. Thank you for continuing to send in signs, rate the signs others have submitted, and write your own funny captions for them at www.signspotting.com. Since launching the website in 2000, we've given away a round-the-world ticket on the Star Alliance to the photographer of the best Signspotting photo of the year as well as $50 to each contributor in the Signspotting books—that's $24,000 to date (plus over $20,000 worth of RTW tickets).

If you like the Signspotting books, you may also enjoy the following:

The Exhibit: The Signspotting Project

Please keep your eyes open for "The Signspotting Project"—one of the funniest exhibits you'll ever see. We enlarged more than 100 of the wackiest sign photos and mounted them back onto real metal signs at approximately life size and put them all